COOKIN' and GRILLIN'

In Alaska *with* SmokeeJo

Including Favorite Fish and Game Recipes from the Lower "48"

Joe Barkoskie

ISBN: 1-4196-6985-0
ISBN13: 978-1419669859
Library of Congress Control Number: 2007905609

Visit www.booksurge.com to order additional copies.

I am excited to share my book of recipes which contains some of the best tastes of Alaska's finest seafood & game.
Along with these I have included my personal favorites from the lower 48 which I have prepared for family, friends & hunting buddies over the years.

I hope that you enjoy them as much as I have!

Fire up that grill! It's time to eat!

SmokeeJo

JOE "SmokeeJo" BARKOSKIE is a lifelong native of Northeast Florida. He grew up in Palm Valley, a rural area roughly 20 miles north of St. Augustine. From the time he was big enough to cast a rod or fire a gun he hunted and fished the local woods and waterways with his father. It was in those early days, helping his dad prepare and cook the game for the family meal, that Joe became interested in cooking. Joe's parents also managed the "Palm Valley Fish Camp" where Joe would listen to the customers tell their fish stories and give their insight into cooking and seasoning. Many years have passed since then and Joe has honed his skills in his own kitchen, taking recipes that have been passed down from generation to generation and experimenting with his own spices and sauces.

Today Joe is heralded throughout the area as the host of hosts and his parties are not to be missed. You can always count on a good time and plenty of good eatin' at SmokeeJo's!

TABLE OF CONTENTS

SALMON RECIPES

Larry Csonka, NFL Hall of Fame and host of Napa's North to Alaska and SmokeeJo with a 52 lb king salmon on the world famous Kenai River in Alaska.

GINGER GLAZED GRILLED SALMON

2 ½ lb salmon steaks-3/4 inch thick
1 tablespoon sesame oil
Salt & pepper to taste

Ginger Butter:

6 tablespoons butter, at room temperature
4 tablespoons ginger preserves
1 teaspoon finely grated lime peel
1 tablespoon snipped chives

Brush the steaks with oil and season with salt and pepper.
Place under a grill 4 inches from the heat and grill four minutes
per side.
Serve with a dollop of ginger butter crowning each steak.

To make the Ginger Butter:
Cream together the ingredients until well mixed. Pack the flavored butter into a crock and refrigerate until needed.

*The butter may be prepared several days in advance.

GRILLED ALASKA SALMON

4 (4 to 6 oz. each) Alaska Salmon steaks or fillets
¼ cup peanut oil
2 tablespoon soy sauce
2 tablespoon balsamic vinegar
2 tablespoon chopped green onions
1 1/2 teaspoon brown sugar
1 clove garlic, minced
¾ teaspoon grated ginger
½ teaspoon red chili flakes
1 tablespoon "*SmokeeJo's Datil Pepper Sauce*" (optional)
½ teaspoon sesame oil
1/8 teaspoon salt

Place salmon steaks or fillets in a glass dish. Whisk together remaining ingredients and pour over salmon. Cover with plastic wrap and marinate in refrigerator 4-6 hours. Remove salmon from marinade and place on a well-oiled grill 5 inches from coals. Grill for 10 minutes per inch of thickness, or until fish just flakes when tested with a fork. Turn halfway through cooking.

GARLIC LOVERS GRILLED SALMON

1 1/2 to 2 lbs. fish fillets
6 to 8 garlic cloves
½ stick of butter
1/8 extra virgin olive oil
½ of a lemon
Paprika or *SmokeeJo's Hungarian Game Spice* if available

Mince the garlic real fine and add the butter and olive oil to a medium frying pan.
Simmer the garlic slowly until it is lightly browned.
Dry fillets, and sprinkle with lemon.
Dip fillets in garlic mixture and let stand for ½ hour.
Get your grill good & hot.
Dust fillets with the paprika.
Place fillets on grill and turn after 4-5 minutes, depending on the thickness

GRILLED SALMON WITH A "KICK"

6 Salmon Fillets
2 tablespoons prepared Horseradish
1 medium Onion (chopped)
3 tablespoons Balsamic Vinegar
2 tablespoons Olive Oil
1 teaspoon Rosemary (chopped)
1 clove Garlic (chopped)
¼ teaspoon salt
1/8 teaspoon freshly ground black pepper
Olive Oil spray

In a blender or food processor, puree Horseradish, Onion, Balsamic vinegar, Oil, Rosemary, and Garlic.
Add Salt and Pepper; blend.
Place each Salmon fillet in center of a piece of heavy-duty aluminum foil sprayed with Olive Oil, spoon 2 tablespoons Horseradish mixture over each Fillet. Bring up edges of each piece of foil and seal, leaving an opening for steam to escape.

Place foil packets in center of cooking grate. Grill 6-10 minutes until fish flakes easily with a fork.

ORIENTAL SALMON SALAD

6 ounces salmon fillets (brushed with oil)
2 tablespoons honey
2 pinches Dry Mustard
2 tablespoons warm water
2 teaspoons soy sauce
1 pinch salt

1 pinch black pepper
Salad Mix (mixed greens)
Roasted sesame seeds

Directions for Honey Mustard Glaze: In a bowl, combine honey, mustard, water, and soy sauce. Add salt & pepper to taste.
Prepare the Salmon Fillet-- Brush salmon fillet lightly with oil, season with salt and pepper.

Grill each side for 2-3 minutes. Cook to desired texture. Brush flesh side of fish with glaze before removing from grill. Serve on top of fresh salad mix. Top with roasted sesame seeds.

SALMON CHILI

16 Ounces of Salmon, Baked, Flaked, Skinned, Boned
2 Cans of Vegetable Chili
1/2 Teaspoon of Ground Cumin
Salt and Pepper to taste
1/2 Cup of Shredded Cheddar Cheese
2 Tablespoons of Diced White Onions
1/2 Cup Roma Tomatoes
1/4 Cup Sour Cream
2 Tablespoons Chopped Cilantro

Remove any Skin, and Bones, from the Salmon if any. Break the Salmon into Chunks. Add Chili to a Saucepan, and then stir in the Salmon and Cumin. Cook until heated through.
Season well with Salt and Pepper.
Divide Chili among 4 Bowls and top each with Cheese, Onions, Tomato, A dollop of Sour Cream, and Cilantro.

GRILLED HONEY LIME SALMON KEBOBS

3 lbs salmon fillet, skin on, cut into 1" chunks
1 green bell pepper, cut into 1" squares
1 red onion, cut into 1" squares
2 cups halved mushrooms
1 lime (juice)
½ cup soy sauce
¼ cup creamed honey
2 garlic cloves, minced
Salt and freshly ground pepper, to taste
12-16 long bamboo skewers, soaked in water

Basting ingredients:
2 limes (juice)
¼ creamed honey

Place salmon and vegetables into a large flat dish. In a small bowl whisk together the lime juice, soy sauce, honey and garlic until honey is dissolved; pour over salmon and vegetables. Season with salt and pepper, toss everything gently together, cover and refrigerate for 6 hours.
Preheat grill to medium-high and oil the grill. Alternate the marinated salmon and vegetables onto the soaked skewers.

In a small bowl, whisk together the lime juice and honey. Place skewers on hot grill and cook ten minutes, basting often with honey mixture and turning once.

GRILLED BLANKET OF SALMON

2 salmon steaks or salmon fillets, 1" thick
4 large romaine lettuce leaves
6 teaspoons olive oil
2 tablespoons capers
4 sprigs of fresh dill
2 lemons- 1 juiced, and 1 sliced thinly
2 piece twine, 3 feet each (or other non flammable)
Salt to taste
Fresh Pepper to taste
Soak twine in hot water for 15 minutes. Rinse salmon in cold water and pat dry with towel.

Repeat the following for each salmon steak. Rinse romaine leaves in water, do not dry. Rub 1 teaspoon of the oil over the inside of each of the lettuce leaves. Place salmon steak in center of one leaf.

Add salt and pepper. Pour 1 teaspoon oil and the juice of ½ lemon over salmon, trapping the juices with the leaf. Top with capers, dill, and one lemon slice.

Place second leaf over salmon, fold ends of bottom leaf up to keep juices trapped, and wrap the string around the leaves to seal. Tie String in a knot.

Place fish on grill over hot coals for 5 minutes. Turn and grill for another 5 minutes. Cooking time will be slightly less for fillets and will vary according to the thickness of the fish.
Cut string and remove top leaf.

SALMON CROQUETTES

½ pound salmon
1 red potato-peeled and chopped
1 shallot-minced
1 egg- beaten
¼ cup Italian seasoned bread crumbs
1 teaspoon dried Italian seasoning
Salt and pepper to taste
½ cup cornflake crumbs
2 tablespoons olive oil

Preheat oven to 350 degrees and lightly grease a small baking dish.

Place salmon in the prepared baking dish, cover, and bake 20 minutes, or until easily flaked with a fork.

Place potato in a small saucepan with enough water to cover, and bring to a boil. Cook until tender. Drain and mash.

In a medium bowl, mix salmon, potato, shallot, egg, and breadcrumbs; Season with Italian seasoning, salt, and pepper. Place the cornflake crumbs in a small bowl. Form the salmon mixture into 1- inch balls, and roll in the cornflakes to coat.

Heat olive oil in a medium saucepan over medium heat. Press the balls into patties, and fry 3 to 5 minutes per side, or until golden brown.

BLACKENED SALMON SANDWICH

4 Alaska Salmon Steaks or Fillet (4-6 oz each), boneless and skinless
4-6 inch French rolls, lightly toasted, remove some of inside breading
1 cup shredded cabbage
8 slices tomato
4 tablespoons mayonnaise
¼ cup plus 1-2 teaspoon *SmokeeJo's Blackening Seasoning*
Oil
Salt & pepper, to taste

Heat a heavy skillet over high heat for 15-20 minutes. Mix mayonnaise with 1-2 teaspoon of blackening seasoning. Test taste, add salt, pepper or more blackening seasoning as necessary; hold aside. Lightly oil both sides of the salmon steaks/fillets and sprinkle with the remaining blackening seasoning. If you prefer hotter add more seasoning.

Place salmon in the hot skillet to blacken; cook 2-3 minutes on the first side, turn and finish cooking. Cooking time will vary based on the thickness of the fish. Spread 1 tablespoon of the mayonnaise mixture onto each French roll. Top each with a blackened salmon fillet, 2 slices of tomato and ¼ cup of the shredded cabbage and serve.

GRILLED SALMON & CABBAGE

4 – 6 oz Salmon fillets (skinned)
2 tablespoons lemon juice
5 garlic cloves (minced)
2 – 8 oz bottles clam juice
1 – 16 oz bag coleslaw
¼ cup cilantro (fresh chopped)
1/8 teaspoon pepper
Heavy duty aluminum foil

Pre-heat your Grill medium to high.

Combine lemon juice, garlic cloves and clam juice in a small saucepan; bring to a boil. Reduce heat; simmer 5 minutes.

Tear off enough aluminum foil to accommodate all 4 fillets, making sure foil is about 4 inches longer than the fish at each end. Place coleslaw on the foil. Arrange the fish on top of the coleslaw.
Pour juice mixture over fish; sprinkle with cilantro and pepper. Bring up sides of foil and double fold. Double fold ends to form a packet, leaving room for heat circulation. Grill on medium to high for 12-15 minutes or until fish flakes easily when tested with a fork.

CEDAR PLANK BOURBON & HERB SALMON

4 Cedar Planks (untreated 12" z 12" soaked in cold water for 3 hours)
4- Salmon Fillets
2 oz Walnut oil
6 Sprigs rosemary or thyme
2 oz Maple Syrup
2 oz Bourbon

Preheat Grill.
Remove the planks from the water and place
on the grill until hot. Brush Board with
walnut oil. Have ready 4 sheets of aluminum foil cut into 16 by 16 inch sheets. Remove the planks with tongs and place 1 plank in the center of each piece of foil. Place salmon on board with the herbs on top. Mix maple syrup and bourbon together and drizzle over salmon. Wrap the aluminum around the salmon, return to the grill and cook for approximately 10 minutes or to medium-well doneness

HAPPY HOUR SALMON

4 Salmon Steaks (about one inch thick)
½ cup vodka
¼ cup fresh orange juice
Juice of 1 lemon
2 tablespoon coarse grained mustard
¼ cup chopped fresh dill
Fresh Orange & Lemon Slices
(sliced thin)

Place steaks in a flat dish in one layer. Combine remaining ingredients and pour over fish, coating on all sides. Marinate at least 20 minutes. Top steaks with fresh slices of orange & lemon and grill steaks in hinged basket over high heat for 5-7 minutes on each side.

DUTCH OVEN SALMON

1-2 Salmon Fillets
Black Pepper
Garlic Powder
1 Lemon (fresh)
4-6 Fresh Mushrooms
4-6 Green Onions
4-8 oz Creamed cheese

Leave skin on the salmon filet.
Slice fillets into wide strips. Place salmon strips, skin side down, into the bottom of a 12" Dutch oven. Sprinkle on black pepper to your taste. Sprinkle on garlic powder to your taste. Cut fresh lemon into quarters and squeeze over salmon strips. Slice fresh mushrooms into thin slices and spread over salmon strips and onto bottom of oven. Slice fresh green onions into thin slices and spread over salmon and onto bottom of oven.

Drop small chunks of creamed cheese onto salmon strips.
Top with lemon slices. Cover Dutch Oven and cook for 15-20 minutes.

CHEESY ITALIAN SALMON BAKE

4- 4-ounce fresh salmon fillets
Nonstick spray coating
1/3 cup light mayonnaise dressing or salad dressing
2 tablespoons grated Parmesan cheese
2 tablespoons snipped fresh chives or sliced green onion
1/2 teaspoon white wine Worcestershire sauce

Rinse fish and pat dry with paper towels. Spray an 8x8x2-inch baking dish with nonstick spray coating; set aside.

In a small bowl stir together mayonnaise dressing, Parmesan cheese, chives or green onion, and Worcestershire sauce. Spread Parmesan mixture over fish fillets.

Bake fish fillets, uncovered, in a 450 ° oven for 12 to 15 minutes or until fish flakes easily when tested with a fork.

CHERYL'S GRILLED SALMON – ANVIK RIVER LODGE

1 lb Salmon Fillet

Marinade:
¼ cup butter
¼ cup olive oil
3 tablespoons soy sauce
1 ½ tablespoons chili sauce
1 tablespoon Worcestershire
1 tablespoon dry mustard
½ tablespoons dry dill
1 ½ tablespoons dry sherry
2 teaspoons lime or lemon juice
2 cloves crushed garlic
Lemon pepper to taste

Combine all ingredients in small saucepan, heat slowly but thoroughly. Brush on salmon ½ hour before grilling and brush on salmon at least one more time during grilling.

When preparing, make an aluminum foil pan by taking three layers of foil and turning up the edges so it forms a flat pan shape with a one inch lip all the way around. Spray the foil with Pam oil spray and put the fillets or steaks on it. No need to skin the salmon first. Then use sauce as directed above. Grill on medium heat for about 15 minutes or until the surface bubbles.

SMOKEEJO'S SMOKED SALMON DIP

6 cups smoked fish
4 Stalks scallions (finely chopped)
½ medium yellow onion (finely chopped)
2 ½ cups mayonnaise
4 oz cream cheese
1 ½ tablespoon Lemon juice
1 teaspoon salt
½ teaspoon cayenne pepper
1 tablespoon Tarragon
½ tablespoon Basil
1 tablespoon Black pepper
1 teaspoon garlic powder
½ teaspoon seasoned salt

Mix all dry ingredients and fish together in a large mixing bowl. Add the scallions and onions and mix well. Add mayonnaise cream cheese and lemon juice until well blended with mixture. Chill in refrigerator for 1 hour. Serve with crackers

BIG RON'S GRILLED MINT SALMON

Salmon Fillets
Lemon Juice
Minced Onion
Butter
Fresh Mint
Aluminum Pan

Melt butter and add lemon & onion. Sauté until onions are almost clear. Pour small amount in the bottom of the aluminum pan. Place fillet in pan and pour remaining mixture on top. Sprinkle with fresh mint. Grill on medium heat until poached consistency.

GRILLED HERB CRUSTED SALMON

12 ounces fresh salmon fillets, 3/4-inch thick
1/3 cup coarsely chopped fresh oregano
1/3 cup coarsely chopped fresh cilantro
1/4 cup sliced green onion
1 clove garlic
1 tablespoon fresh lemon juice
2 teaspoons olive oil
1/4 teaspoon salt
1/8 teaspoon pepper

Rinse fish; pat dry with paper towels. Cut into two (6-ounce) pieces. Set aside.
In the bowl of a food processor or a mini-chopper combine oregano, cilantro, green onion, garlic, lemon juice, oil, salt, and pepper. Cover and process until chopped. (Or, use a knife to finely chop oregano, cilantro, green onion, and garlic. Transfer to a shallow bowl. Stir in lemon juice, oil, salt, and pepper.) Generously coat both sides of salmon with the herb mixture.
Cook the salmon on the rack of an uncovered grill directly over medium-hot coals for 6 to 8 minutes or until the salmon just begins to flake easily with a fork. To serve, cut each salmon piece in half.

GRILLED MEXICAN STYLE SALMON

4 Salmon Steaks, 6-8 oz. each
Fresh lime Slices for garnish

Marinade:
4 Garlic Cloves, finely chopped
2 tablespoons Extra Virgin Olive Oil

Juice of 2 Limes
1/4-1/2 teaspoon SmokeeJo's Datil Pepper Sauce (or more to taste, if you like spicy hot)
¼ teaspoon Ground Cumin
Pinch of Allspice
Pinch of Cinnamon
Pinch of White Sugar
Salt & Pepper to taste

Combine all marinade ingredients in a med. Bowl and mix well. Place Salmon in a shallow, non metallic dish and pour marinade over top. Turn fish to coat, cover with plastic wrap and refrigerate at least 1 hour, or overnight. Cook over hot coals about 4-5 min. on each side. Top with fresh lime slices.

SMOKED SALMON

6-8 pounds Salmon Filets
Ingredients for Brine: ½ cup salt
1 cup brown sugar
 1 cup white sugar
(Mix more if needed, depends on amount & size of filets)

Wash Filets thoroughly, then pat dry. In a large stainless steel pan or ice chest place one layer of filets on the bottom. Coat filets thoroughly with brine mixture. With your next filets, coat the meat side with the brine and place on top of filets in the pan, meat to meat.
Keep repeating this process always making sure that your layers are meat to meat.
Cover pan and refrigerate for 8-12 hours or overnight. If you have them in a cooler just sprinkle ice over the top to keep them cool.

Next step:

Remove fish and rinse thoroughly, over and over until water is clear.

Lay filets on newspaper or old towels and pat dry.

Let air dry for 4-6 hours until meat is "tacky" or dry.

*note: if humidity is high, place a fan to blow directly on the fish to help the drying process.

I have to do this in Florida.

 Last step:

Place the filets on racks in smoker and smoke for 8-10 hours (depending on the thickness of the filets) @ 180 degrees or low heat.

*Tip: I like to rub a little brown sugar on filets just before smoking

*note: if you are going to use a grill, cook at low heat for 2-3 hours.

"*BREWSKY*" BATTERED SALMON STICKS

1 lb salmon fillet, sliced into strips-6inches in length and 1 inch thick

"*Brewsky Batter*":

4 tablespoons flour

4 tablespoons corn starch

1 teaspoon lemon pepper

1 teaspoon sugar

Beer (I prefer Bud)

Mix the dry ingredients in a mixing bowl with enough beer to make a batter a little thin. You want it thinner than pancake batter. Dip the sliced fillets into the batter and deep fry until the batter turns a golden brown. Drain on paper towels and serve with "*SmokeeJo's*" *Datil Pepper Cocktail Sauce*"!

Ingredients for cocktail sauce:

4 oz. of mayonnaise

SmokeeJo's Datil Pepper Sauce (to taste)

HALIBUT RECIPES

Larry Csonka and Audrey Bradshaw hosts of Napa's North to Alaska with their catch of halibut in Southeast Alaska.

POOR MAN'S LOBSTER

2 lbs Halibut Fillets
¼ lb butter
One lemon
1 tablespoon Minced garlic
20 oz bottle of 7 up

Cube the Halibut into approximately 1 inch cubes, set aside. In a medium sauce pan bring the 7-up to boil. Melt butter and minced garlic together, set aside.

When the 7 up is at a brisk boil, place the cubes of Halibut 4-5 pieces at a time to keep temperature even, when the Halibut begin to float off the bottom, remove them from the heat. Serve with Drawn butter and a squeeze of lemon

GRILLED HALIBUT TACOS

2/3 cup Lime juice
½ cup chopped green onions
2 tablespoons vegetable oil
2 tablespoons minced fresh cilantro
2 tablespoons chopped seeded jalepeno peppers
1 pkg taco seasoning
4 halibut steaks
8 bacon strips
Shredded lettuce
Shredded cheddar cheese
1 cup diced tomatoes
Taco shells (or you can also use tortillas)
SmokeeJo's Datil pepper sauce

In a large Ziploc bag, combine the first 6 ingredients. Add halibut; seal the bag and turn to coat. Refrigerate for 10-15 minutes, turning once.
In a large skillet, cook bacon over medium heat until cooked but not crisp. Drain on paper towels.
Drain and discard the marinade from halibut.
Wrap two slices of bacon over the top and sides of each steak; secure with soaked wooden toothpicks.
Spray your grill with nonstick cooking spray before grilling. Place halibut with the bacon side down on grill rack. Grill the halibut, covered, over medium heat for 4-6 minutes on each side or until fish flakes easily with a fork. Discard the toothpicks.
Cut the steaks into medium to thin strips.
Place 2-3 halibut strips into each taco shell, following cheese, and shredded lettuce & top with pepper sauce.
"

Umm.Umm..Umm"

GRILLED HALIBUT & DUNGENESS CRAB TOPPING

2-One pound Halibut fillets.
1 cup Dungeness crab Meat
Unsalted butter to sauté crab

Marinade;
½ cup Honey
1 cup lemon juice
¼ cup brown sugar

The special sauce:
8 oz. can Crushed pineapple (drained)
2 tablespoon shallots (chopped)
1 tablespoon ginger minced
2 teaspoon fresh Cilantro (chopped)
2 teaspoon Lemon Juice
1teaspoon non-pareil Capers
¼ teaspoon Tabasco Sauce

Directions:

Mix the marinade in a small bowl. Rub the halibut fillets with the marinade. Place the fillets in the refrigerator for an hour.
Remove about 15 minutes before you are ready to grill.

Brush Fillets with Marinade and grill halibut a few minutes on each side. Cook until fillets are opaque and flake easily with a fork.

Lightly sauté the crab meat in the unsalted butter.

Place the halibut on a serving platter, top with sautéed crab meat and then the sauce.

"SMOKEEJO'S" HUNGARIAN HALIBUT

1 ½ pound Halibut – 1 inch thick
½ cup Nonfat Yogurt
½ cup Light sour cream
2 tablespoons All-purpose flour
1 teaspoon SmokeeJo's Hungarian Game Spice (or you can just use paprika)
1 ½ cup Fresh mushrooms sliced
½ cup Chopped onion
2 tablespoons Butter
1/3 cup Dry white wine
1 teaspoon Dried dill weed
½ teaspoon Salt
Hot cooked egg noodles (buttered)

Remove any skin and bones from the halibut. Cut fish into 1-inch cubes. Set aside. In a small bowl stir together yogurt, sour cream, flour, and Hungarian game spice. Set aside.

In a skillet cook mushrooms and onion in hot butter until tender. Add fish, wine, dill weed and salt. Bring just to boiling then reduce heat. Simmer, covered, about 5 minutes, or until the fish just flakes. Remove the fish and mushrooms. Stir the yogurt mixture into the skillet, cook and stir until it is thickened and bubbly. Cook 1 minute more.
Return fish and mushrooms to sauce, heat through. Serve over egg noodles.

SWEET FRIED HALIBUT

4 halibut Fillets
1 egg
1 tablespoon honey
1 cup crushed Saltine Crackers
½ cup flour
½ teaspoon salt
¼ teaspoon pepper
Oil

In shallow bowl, beat egg and honey.
In a separate bowl, mix cracker crumbs, flour, salt, and pepper.
Dip fish in egg, then crumbs.
In a large skillet heat ¼ inch oil.
Fry fish on medium to high heat for 3-4 minutes a side.

MACADAMIA NUT HALIBUT

1-2 Halibut Fillets (the thinner fillets work best)
1 cup Macadamia nuts (chopped fine)
Salt
Pepper
SmokeeJo's Blackening Seasoning (optional)
1-2 eggs (whipped)
Vegetable or Peanut Oil
Chop nuts in food processor. Whip eggs in bowl.
Cover bottom of the pan with oil and heat to low-medium. Be careful not to get it to hot.
Season fish, dip into egg wash. Place fillet in nuts and cover well on both sides.
Place fillets in pan and fry on low-medium for 1-2 minutes per side.

* **Note:** *If you have thick fillets, just brown well on each side and place in oven on cookie sheet for about 5 minutes at 350 degrees to finish cooking*

HEARTY HALIBUT STEW

2 lbs of Halibut (cut into 1 inch cubes)
3 medium potatoes-peeled and cubed (small and pre-cooked)
1 large yellow onion
1 small bell pepper-diced
3 cloves garlic-diced
4 strips of bacon (fried crispy)
1 16 oz can cream of mushroom soup
1 16 oz can cream of celery soup
1 tablespoon "SmokeeJo's Hungarian Style Game Spice
Salt and pepper (to taste)
½-1 cup of water (to desired consistency)

In an 8-quart pot, fry the bacon until crispy.
Take bacon out and set aside.
On low heat, cook onions, bell peppers, and garlic in bacon grease until soft.
Add cream of mushroom, and cream of celery soup and water.
To avoid scorching, bring to a simmer stirring frequently.
Add Halibut and seasonings. Bring back to simmer stirring frequently for about 10 minutes.
Add potatoes and heat through for about 5 minutes

HALIBUT HUSH PUPPIES

Fresh Halibut Fillet's (Cut into ½ to ¾ cubes)
1 tablespoon Old bay seasoning
1 package of dry hush puppy mix w/onions (I prefer House Autrey)
Vegetable oil

Heat the oil in a deep fryer.
Prepare the hush puppy mix as directed on the package then add ½ cup additional water. You want the batter to be a bit thinner than normal.
Sprinkle lightly with the Old Bay seasoning.
Dip into hush puppy mix then drop into the hot oil.
Fry for 2-3 minutes, or until golden brown.
Drain real well on paper towel and serve

MARINATED BARBECUE HALIBUT

2 lbs Halibut fillets
¼ Cup Orange Juice
¼ cup Soy Sauce
2 tablespoons Ketchup
2 tablespoons Chopped Fresh Parsley
2 tablespoons Salad oil
1 tablespoon Lemon juice
½ teaspoon Oregano
½ teaspoon Pepper
1 Clove of Garlic

Place fillets in a single layer in a shallow pan. Combine the remaining ingredients, mix well and pour over the fish. Marinate for 30 minutes, turning the fillets once or twice to be sure they are well coated. Reserve the sauce.
Grill fish about 3-5 minutes on each side, depending on the thickness. Pour remaining sauce over fillets before serving.

HALIBUT OLYMPIA

2 lbs Halibut fillets
1 cup mayonnaise
1 cup fresh Parmesan cheese or mix Parmesan and Ricotta
1 thinly sliced large white onion
2 teaspoon real lemon juice
Garlic salt, pepper

Mix mayonnaise, cheese & spices to taste. Add lemon juice.
Put a layer of onions on the bottom of a casserole dish.
Lay Halibut fillets on top of the onions.
Add another layer of onions on the fillets.
Seal Halibut and onions with mayonnaise mixture.
Cover and bake at 350 degrees for 25-30 minutes (depends on fillet size).
Remove cover and broil for approximately 7 minutes or until browned on top.

*Amount of ingredients varies depending on how much Halibut you are using.

Manhattan-Style Halibut Chowder

2 tablespoons butter
2 ¾ cups chopped onion
1 cup chopped carrot
¾ cup chopped celery
3 garlic cloves, minced
¼ cup tomato paste
1 cup dry white wine
2 cups chopped peeled red potato
2 cups water
1 tablespoon chopped fresh or 1 teaspoon dried thyme
1 teaspoon salt
½ teaspoons freshly ground black pepper
2 (8-ounce) bottles clam juice
1(28 ounce) can diced tomatoes, undrained
1 bay leaf
2 pounds halibut fillets, skinned and cut into 1-inch pieces

Melt butter in a Dutch oven over medium-high heat. Add onion, carrot, celery, and garlic to pan; sauté 10 minutes or until lightly browned. Stir in tomato paste; cook 1 minute. Stir in wine; cook 1 minute. Add potato and next 7 ingredients; bring to a boil. Reduce heat; simmer 30 minutes.
Add fish. Cover and simmer 10 minutes or until fish flakes easily when tested with a fork.

GRILLED HALIBUT WITH CRAB MEAT STUFFING

4 Halibut fillets cut in half-1-1/2 inches thick
½ cup olive oil
SmokeeJo's Hungarian game spice seasoning (or your favorite)
Crab meat stuffing

Crab Meat Stuffing
1- cup crabmeat
2 tablespoons minced red pepper
2 tablespoons minced green onion
2 tablespoons chopped celery
¼-cup butter (melted)
1 ½ cups soft white bread cubes
1 tablespoon lemon juice

Mix all of the above ingredients and set aside.
Pre-heat grill.
Dip each fillet in olive oil.
Sprinkle with seasoning
Lay on aluminum foil.
Place stuffing on one fillet.
Take other fillet and place on top (make a sandwich)
Wrap in aluminum foil.
Repeat with other fillet.
Place on grill for 15 to 20 minutes.

"SALT & VINEGAR" FRIED HALIBUT

Halibut fillets cut ½ inch thick
1 bag of Salt and Vinegar Chips
1 can of beer at room temperature (I prefer Budweiser)
Oil

Soak the fillets in the beer. Crush the salt and vinegar chips up real fine.
Coat the beer soaked fillets in the chips until well coated. Place in very hot oil and fry until the fish becomes a golden brown.

TROUT RECIPES

GRILLED TROUT & "SHROOMS"

4 Trout Fillets
8 oz Fresh Portabella mushrooms, sliced
2 tablespoons Balsamic vinegar
2 tablespoons Olive Oil
1 teaspoon Italian Seasoning
¼ teaspoon salt

Preheat Grill to medium-high/ Center one fish on each sheet of aluminum foil. In a bowl, combine remaining ingredients. Let stand 5 minutes. Spoon ¼ of the mixture over each fish steak. Bring up sides of foil and double fold. Double fold ends to form a packet. Repeat to make 4 packets. Grill 12 to 14 minutes on medium-high in covered grill.

"CHEESY GRILLED TROUT"

Marinade:
1/2 cup Extra Virgin Olive Oil
4 tablespoons of Fresh lemon juice
1 1/2 cup White wine
3 Garlic cloves; minced
4 tablespoons of Fresh parsley; minced

8 10 oz trout; heads/tails on
1 Onion; sliced thin
Salt & pepper; to taste
1/4 lb Parmesan cheese; grated
1/4 lb Romano cheese; grated
Marinade: Combine all ingredients for marinade and then divide between two large zip-lock bags. Place zip-locks in large bowl and add 4 trout to each bag. Seal them tightly. Turn a few times to make sure all fish surfaces touch marinade. Let them sit at room temperature for 1 hour. Remove fish from marinade and salt and pepper each liberally inside and out. Arrange fish on greased foil paced on prepared grill. Sprinkle fish with cheese and press to adhere to fish. Cook for about 6-8 minutes or until fish flakes.

GRILLED TROUT IN A BLANKET

3 lb Trout (Whole)
¾ cup melted butter
1 package dry onion soup mix
1 tablespoon SmokeeJo's Hungarian Game Spice (optional)
½ pound of bacon

Combine butter, soup mix, game spice & pepper. Spread Trout with mixture and wrap bacon slices around it. Secure with toothpicks. Grill 10 minutes per side or until meat flakes easily.

TROUT IN A SKILLET

3 lb trout (cut into 6 pieces)
1 large onion
2 tablespoons flour
1 ½ cup of beer
2 tablespoons brown sugar
Pepper
2 teaspoons Worcestershire sauce
4 tablespoons vegetable oil

In a large skillet, sauté diced onion in hot oil until it becomes trans-lucent. Add the flour to onions and stirring constantly, cook for 2 minutes. Add the beer, brown sugar, pepper, and Worcestershire sauce to the skillet and heat until the sauce thickens. Stir constantly. Place the fish pieces in the skillet. Cook until the fish flakes easily with a fork.

CAJUN FRIED TROUT

2 cups all-purpose flour
3 teaspoons salt
2 teaspoons Cajun seasoning
1-1/2 teaspoons pepper
1/8 - teaspoon ground cinnamon

2 lbs trout fillets
2 eggs
¼ cup water
2 cups mashed potato flakes
6 teaspoons vegetable oil

Combine the first 5 ingredients in a large zip-lock bag. Shake real well.
Add the fillets one at a time and shake to coat. Whisk eggs and water in a bowl. Place potato flakes in another bowl.

Dip each coated fillet into the egg mixture, then coat in the potato flakes repeat with each fillet twice.

In a large skillet, heat 3-4 tablespoons oil over medium-high heat. Cook fish in small batches (2-3 at a time) for 3-4 minutes n each side or until the fish flakes easily with a fork. You can add oil as needed

3 lbs of trout cut into 1 inch cubes
Seafood breader mix (my personal favorite is "House Autry")
1 12 ouch beer of your choice (mine would be BW)
2 eggs
Salt
Pepper

Old bay seasoning
Lemon juice
Vegetable oil

Mix beer, eggs, & a tablespoon of lemon juice.
Mix Breader mix, Old bay, and salt & pepper.
Dip trout into egg then into breader, repeat this one more time.
Drop into deep fryer. Fry until golden brown.

GRILLED TROUT IN A BASKET

2 Whole Trout (split down the back)
1 green pepper (sliced)
1 yellow pepper (sliced)
1 yellow onion (sliced)
Lemon and Dill seasoning
Salt
Pepper
Lemon Juice
Olive Oil

Season both whole trout thoroughly with lemon dill, salt and pepper.
Sprinkle with lemon juice.
Pour a little olive oil on a paper towel and lightly dab on fish.
Place the sliced peppers and onions on top of fish.
Place in grilling basket and close tightly.
Place on hot grill for approximately 2-3 minutes on each side until browned and fish flakes easily.

GRILLED TROUT WITH CITRUS AND CILANTRO

4 boned whole fresh trout (about 10 ounces each)
2 tablespoons olive oil
Salt and freshly ground pepper
8 thin orange slices
8 thin lemon slices
8 thin lime slices
¼ cup chopped fresh cilantro or parsley, plus sprigs for garnish

Prepare a medium fire in a covered charcoal or gas grill. Oil the grill rack. Brush the trout inside and out with the olive oil.
Season the trout with the salt and pepper. Laying the trout open, overlap 1 each of the orange, lemon, and lime slices along one side. Sprinkle each with 1 tablespoon of the chopped cilantro, and then fold the trout over to enclose the filling. Secure the opening with small skewers or wooden toothpicks. Grill the trout for 5 minutes. Use a wide spatula to turn it carefully. Grill 4-5 minutes longer, until just cooked through. Serve garnished with the remaining citrus slices and cilantro sprigs

SMOKEEJO'S PALM VALLEY STYLE FRIED RAINBOW TROUT

6 Rainbow Trout fillets
Cornmeal mix
SmokeeJo's Datil Pepper Sauce (Or Hot sauce of choice)
Vegetable Oil

Place fillets in shallow bowl and cover with hot sauce
Dredge fillets in cornmeal mix until coated.
Drop in oil (350 degrees)
Drain fillets on paper towels.

HOT GRILLED TROUT

4 Trout (about 1lb each)
2 tablespoon of Parsley (chopped)
2 tablespoon of Sesame Seeds
½ teaspoon of Ground Ginger
½ teaspoon of Salt
¼ cup of lemon juice
1 tablespoon of "SmokeeJo's Datil Pepper Sauce"
2 tablespoon of margarine (melted)
1 tablespoon of vegetable oil

In shallow dish, combine lemon juice, margarine, oil parsley, sesame seeds, hot sauce, ginger and salt; mix well
Pierce skin of fish in several places with tines of fork. Roll fish in juice mixture to coat inside and out. Cover. Refrigerate 30 minutes to 1 hour, turning occasionally. Remove fish from marinade; reserve marinade. Place fish in hand-held hinged grill; brush fish with marinade, cook 5 minutes longer. Fish is done when it flakes easily with fork. If desired, serve with additional hot sauce.

TERIYAKI TROUT KABOBS

Ingredients: 3 lbs. trout filets
1 can of (16 oz) pineapple chunks
1 green pepper, cut into 1" squares

Marinade
1 teaspoon ground ginger
¼ cup reserved pineapple juice
1 teaspoon dry mustard
½ cup soy sauce
1 clove garlic, crushed
2 tbs brown sugar
¼ cup sherry

Directions: Cut fillets into one-inch cubes. Drain pineapple
Reserving ¼ cup of the liquid. Combine the pineapple juice, soy sauce, sherry, brown
sugar, ginger, mustard and garlic.

Pour marinade over fish; cover and refrigerate for at Least 1 hour, longer is better.

Drain fish and reserve marinade. Thread fish, pineapple chunks, and green peppers
Alternately on skewers.

Cook 4-5 inches from hot coals for 4-5 minutes.
Baste frequently with marinade. Turn and cook 4-5 minutes longer or until fish is flakey

DUTCH OVEN TROUT

6-8 inch trout
12 slices of bacon
1 teaspoon garlic powder
1 teaspoon ground pepper

Filet the trout, Lay three slices of bacon on the bottom of a Dutch Oven, up ½ a trout flesh-side-down, on each slice. Sprinkle pepper & garlic powder lightly over upper sides of fish. Arrange a second layer of bacon and fish at right angles to the first, and continue to arrange other layer, each at right angles to one below it, until all the fish halves are in. Cover the Dutch Oven, bury in coals, cook 35-40 minutes. Serve a slice of bacon with each half fish.

*This is especially good with a bowl of hot grits!

ROCKFISH, LING COD AND PIKE RECIPES

With a beautiful background of the Susitna River, cameramen John Dietrich and Pat Smith capture on film what "SmokeeJo" does best, cook!

CHEESE GRILLED LING COD

Ingredients
4 fish steaks or fillets (1 1/2 lb)
1/2 small onion, skinned and grated
4 oz of cheese, grated
2 oz. butter
1 teaspoon dry mustard
salt and pepper
2 tomatoes, sliced

In bowl mix together the onions, cheese, butter, dry mustard & salt & pepper until well blended.
Place the steaks on the grill rack and grill under a medium heat for about 5 minutes turn them and grill for a further 3 minutes.
Spread the cheese mixture over the fish and lay 1-2 slices of tomato on each steak.
Grill for a final 3-5 minutes, until the cheese topping is golden and the tomatoes are cooked.

BLACKENED LING COD

Heat cast iron skillet at least 10 minutes. (The hotter the better)
Melt 1 and ¾ cup unsalted butter in separate pan. Reserve ¾ to serve
with fish. Dip filets in melted butter coating both sides well.
Sprinkle blackening evenly on both sides. Cook quickly over high
Heat until underside forms a nice crust (approx. 1 minute). Turn over
and repeat, being careful not to burn.
Serve with butter.

*Tip: It is best to use filets that are about 1 to 1 ½ inch thick.

GRILLED BLACKENED BLACK "BASS" ROCKFISH

1 teaspoon SmokeeJo's Blackening seasoning
1/2 teaspoon garlic salt
1/4 teaspoon onion powder
1/8 teaspoon black pepper
1/8 teaspoon cayenne pepper
1/2 cup olive or canola oil
4 6 ounce halibut steaks

Blend all seasonings with oil and pour into gallon size zip-lock plastic bag. Add Rockfish, turning over to coat on all sides. Refrigerate fish while heating grill.
Heat heavy duty skillet or range top. Sear seafood, about 15 to 30 seconds on each side. Remove to platter. Transfer seafood to oiled hot grill. Turn once, basting with remaining marinade; cook about 6 to 12 minutes per inch of thickness.

MESQUITE-GRILLED MARGARITA PIKE

1 Fresh Pike (any size, 3-4 pounds is best)
2-3 Tablespoons olive oil
Lime Juice from ¼ fresh lime
Splash of Tequila
Garlic powder
Chile powder
Cumin
Fresh cilantro
Salt & pepper to taste
Hot pepper flakes
Mesquite Chips

Coat both sides of the filets with oil. Squeeze half of the lime juice on each fillet. Sprinkle rib cage side with tequila and the remainder of the above listed ingredients.
Allow to marinate for about an hour. Fire up your grill. When the fire is hot, add the wet mesquite chips. When things get good and smoky, lay the pike fillets on the grill rib cage side down. Cook for 2-3 minutes, turn and cook for another 2-3 minutes. Do not overcook. The fillets should still be moist and tender. Serve with Spanish rice

FRIED "PICKLED" PIKE

2 lbs Pike fillets
1 egg
2 tablespoons dill pickle juice
Salt
Lemon pepper
1 cup instant mashed potato flakes

Beat egg, pickle juice, salt, and lemon pepper. Dip fish in mixture, then coat with potato flakes. Fry 3-5 minutes on each side or until brown.

SMOKEEJO'S BEER BATTERED SHEE FISH

2 lbs Shee Fish Fillets
1 cup plain flour
1 teaspoon black pepper
1 teaspoon salt
1 teaspoon baking powder
½ teaspoon dried dill weed
¾ cup beer
½ cup milk
2 eggs
A dash of hot sauce (optional)
Vegetable oil

In a large bowl, mix together flour, salt, pepper, baking powder, and dill. Add beer, milk, hot sauce and eggs; mix well. Place fish Fillets in batter mixture, coat well, and let stand for 15 minutes. In a deep fryer, heat oil to 375. Place fish strips in hot oil, and fry until golden brown.

PARMESAN FRIED PIKE

1 lb fish fillets
¼ cup flour
Dash of garlic salt
1 beaten egg
¼ cup milk
½ Cup saltine crackers, finely crushed
2 tablespoons Parmesan cheese
2 tablespoons parsley, finely snipped
½ cup oil
Lemon slices and parsley sprigs for garnish

Rinse fillets and pat dry with paper towel
Combine flour and garlic salt; set aside. Blend egg and milk. Set aside.
Combine cracker crumbs, Parmesan and parsley. Coat the fish with flour mixture. Dip in egg mixture, then coat with crumb mixture.
In skillet cook fish in single layer, in hot oil. Fry 4-5 minutes per side, until the fish browns and flakes easily. Drain on paper towel. Serve garnished with lemon slices and parsley sprigs.

GAME RECIPES

THE CAMP" DINNER"

2 lbs ground moose
1 teaspoon salt
1 teaspoon pepper
1 teaspoon garlic powder
1 head of cabbage
3 cups carrots- peeled and shredded
4 cups potatoes- shredded
1 large onion- sliced
6 slices Velveeta cheese

Pre-heat oven to 350 degrees
Season ground moose with salt, pepper and garlic powder.
Mix well. Form into patties.

Place each patty on one cabbage leaf on a double sheet of foil.
Divide carrots, potatoes, onion and cheese slices evenly over patties and top each with another cabbage leaf.

Seal foil around each patty and bake 30-40 minutes.

DUTCH OVEN MOOSE STEAKS

1 - 1 1/2 lb. Moose steaks
2-3 medium potatoes, shredded
2 green peppers, sliced
2 tablespoon bacon grease
4-5 medium carrots, shredded

1/2 c. water
8 strips bacon, crisp and crumbled
4 onions, sliced

Light 25 briquettes to red hot. Cut moose steaks into individual sized servings. Place in a heavy-duty plastic bag with a few teaspoon flour and pound until thin. Cook bacon in Dutch oven over 10-12 coals, leaving bacon grease on bottom. Brown steak with bacon grease, on one side until brown. Turn over and quickly brown other side. While meat is cooking, place equal amounts of vegetables on top of each steak piece, peppers and onions on top. Add salt and pepper if desired. Pour in water, cover and simmer. Leave 5 coals below and place 12-15 coals on top of oven. Steam until vegetables are tender, 15-20 minutes. When done, remove steak together with vegetables as a single stack.

GRILLED CARIBOU STEAKS TOPPED WITH ONION

*Prepare the onions 1 hour before grilling the steaks

Onion Wrap
4-6 large sweet onions
4-6 beef bouillon cubes
½ stick of butter
Foil
Peel and clean the onion real well. Cut out a core at the top of the onion. Place the bouillon cube in first and then top it with a small square of butter. Wrap tightly in aluminum foil. Grill on medium-slow coals for 1-2 hours.

*Note: These may also be done in the oven @ 400 degrees for 1 hour.

CARIBOU STEAKS

4-6 Caribou Steaks (1/2 inch slices)

Marinade: 1 cup of Jack Daniels
½ cup brown sugar
¼ cup soy sauce

Slice meat in ½ inch slices. Marinade for 6 hours. Cook over medium coals until cooked as desired. Top the steaks with the grilled onion & you are good to go! Um..Um..Um..

CRUSTY FRIED CARIBOU

1 Caribou tenderloin (cut into 1 inch slices)
2 eggs
Salt
Pepper
Your favorite seasoning
Saltine Cracker (or crackers of choice) Crushed fine
Cooking oil
Beat eggs.
Season the meat. Mix meat into egg wash and set aside.
Crush the crackers real fine in bag or if available a food processor.
Heat oil to 325 degrees.
Coat meat well with cracker crumbs and fry until golden brown.

CARIBOU SLOPPY "SMOKEEJO'S"

2 lbs ground caribou
1 jar mild picante sauce (8oz)
1 cup diced onion
¼ cup white vinegar
1 cup green pepper, diced
1 package of Taco seasoning
¼ cup of brown sugar
¼ cup green chilies diced and drained

Brown ground caribou in a skillet with onion and drain on paper towels.
Return mixture to skillet and add green pepper, taco seasoning, brown sugar, chilies, picante sauce and white vinegar. Cover and simmer 1 hour until thickened. Serve on hamburger rolls.

FRIED PTARMIGAN

4 Ptarmigan breasts-cut into finger strips
1 cup of self rising flour
Garlic powder
Black pepper
½ cup soy sauce
Cooking oil

Mix flour, garlic powder & pepper in a bowl.
Dip ptarmigan strips into seasoned flour, then into the soy sauce.
Deep fry strips in cooking oil until golden brown.

MOOSE SALTIMBOCA- "JUMP IN YOUR MOUTH"

6 moose tenderloin steaks (sliced 1 inch thick)
1 Bag of Fresh Spinach
6 Thin slices of prosciutto
12 small sage leaves
Flour
8-10 tablespoons of butter
4 hardboiled eggs (peeled & sliced)
Marsala Wine
Milk
2 Coves fresh garlic (pressed)
Toothpicks

In a shallow pan, place moose steaks and cover with milk. Place in the refrigerator overnight.

Clean the leaves of the spinach away from the large stems and rinse in colander. Let most of the water drain off.

Cover the bottom of a large pan with olive oil and heat, adding the garlic as it heats. Brown garlic then remove it from the pan. Now wilt the spinach in the olive oil. Turn off heat. (Do not over cook spinach)

On Top of each slice of moose place one piece of prosciutto and two sage leaves. Fold in half and secure with a toothpick.

Melt the butter in a large frying pan. Dust the meat in flour and brown in the butter on both sides (Do not over cook). Remove meat from the pan and remove the toothpick. Open the meat up.

Completely de-glaze the pan with a good amount of Marsala wine and let simmer for a moment.

Plate the Moose steaks, top with spinach and a couple of slices of egg. Pour the sauce from the de-glazed pan over the meat and ENJOY!

GARLIC GRILLED PTARMIGAN ON A STICK

3 garlic cloves, crushed
2 tablespoons honey
4 tablespoons tomato ketchup
4 tablespoons Worcestershire sauce
2 tablespoons English or Dijon mustard
2 teaspoons SmokeeJo's Datil Pepper Sauce
3 skinless, boneless Ptarmigan breasts
Salt and freshly ground black pepper
Bamboo skewers 12-(10 inch)

Soak bamboo skewers in water for 20 minutes.

Meanwhile, mix together the garlic, honey, ketchup, Worcestershire sauce, mustard and hot pepper sauce. Season to taste with the salt and freshly ground black pepper.
Toss in the Ptarmigan breasts and stir until well combined. Transfer to a nonmetallic dish, cover and marinate for 20 minutes or 30 minutes, or even overnight.

Prepare grill, Thread the marinated Ptarmigan onto the skewers. Cook over the hot coals of an outdoor grill for 5 to 60 minutes.

The Lower "48" Recipes
Fish, Game and Some of my Personal Favorites

SmokeeJo with a big Redfish on the Intracoastal Waterway in St. Augustine, Florida.

GRILLED "ORIENTAL" TUNA

Fresh Tuna

Marinade:
2 Parts Sesame Oil
1 Part Soy Sauce
2 Parts Ginger Dressing

Sauce: (mix all of these ingredients and put in fridge)
1 cup Mayonnaise
2 tablespoons Wasabee Dressing
2 tablespoons Soy Sauce
1 tablespoon Lemon Juice
½ teaspoon Ground Ginger Paste
½ teaspoon Garlic Paste

Directions:
Marinate Tuna for 30 minutes.
Sear to medium on grill
(or cast iron skillet)
Pour Sauce on plates
Place Tuna on top of sauce.

SMOKEEJO'S GRILLED KINGFISH

6 Kingfish Fillet's (skin on)
¼ cup lemon juice
½ cup Worcestershire Sauce
1 cup Italian dressing
Splash of Soy sauce
Black pepper
Garlic & herb seasoning

Place fillets in large ziploc bag, or baking pan.
Mix together lemon juice, Worcestershire sauce, Italian dressing and soy sauce.
Pour marinade over fillets and place in refrigerator for 1 1/2 to 2 hours.
Remove fillets from marinade and season with black pepper and garlic & lemon herb seasoning.
Place on grill for 45 minutes to 1 hour depending on thickness.
If using a *gas grill*: Pre-heat on high. When ready for fillets turn to low.
If using a *charcoal grill*: Build coals on one end of grill and place fillets on opposite end.

GRILLED MARGARITA GROUPER

1 ½ lbs grouper fillets
1/3 cup white or gold tequila
½ cup triple sec
¾ cup fresh lime juice
1 teaspoon salt
2-3 large fresh garlic cloves, crushed
2 teaspoon vegetable oil
3 medium tomatoes, diced
1 medium sweet onion, finely chopped
1 tablespoon minced datil pepper or pepper of choice
2-4 tablespoon chopped fresh cilantro
1 pinch sugar
Ground black pepper

Combine tequila, triple sec, lime juice, garlic, salt, and oil.
Place fish in single layer in a flat dish. Pour tequila mixture over, and marinate for ½ hour at room temperature, or 3 hours in the refrigerator.
Just before serving, combine tomatoes, onion, chile, cilantro, sugar, and salt to taste to make fresh tomato salsa.
Remove fish from marinade (reserve), and pat dry. Brush fish on both sides with oil, and grind black pepper over it.
Cook on greased grill over high heat (about 4 minutes per side).
Boil marinade in a saucepan for about two minutes, remove and discard the garlic cloves, and spoon over fish.
Serve alongside fresh tomato salsa.

*Tip- Wipe down grill with olive oil to grease grill

Game Cooking Tips

To freeze wild birds, I place them in a tightly sealed plastic container or heavy duty Ziploc bag and fill with water covering them completely.
This helps prevent freezer burn when storing birds for cooking later.

With wild birds, which are very lean, you will get added flavor and moistness by placing bacon or pork on the breasts before cooking.

With Venison, you can just add a little meat tenderizer and use any of your favorite beef recipes. Ground Venison is a favorite with all ground beef recipes. It is lower in calories, fat and cholesterol than most meat.

For better tasting game, keep meats clean and cool after field dressing using a damp towel or cloth to wipe down. Allow air to circulate the meat, even during transporting.

GRILLED "COLA" VENISON TENDERLOIN

Venison Tenderloin cut 1" thick

Marinade:
2 cups of cola
1 cup mustard
Dash of Hungarian Game Spice
SmokeeJo's Datil Pepper Sauce for dipping

Marinate meat for one hour.
On medium heat grill 2-3 minutes on each side for medium well.

GRILLED DEER STEAKS

4 Venison Steak Tenderloin (3/4 inch thick)

Marinade:
½ Cup soy sauce
½ cup Italian dressing
1 to 2 tablespoons of A-1 Steak sauce
½ teaspoon Hickory liquid smoke
Pinch of salt and pepper
1-2 clove of garlic minced

Place steak tenderloins in shallow pan or Ziploc bag and pour marinade over meat.
Marinate in refrigerator for 2 hours.
Grill over hot coals 5 minutes on each side

GRILLED STUFFED ELK TENDERLOIN

1-3lb Elk tenderloin
½ pound of sausage
1-cup salsa
Italian Dressing

Trim loin and cut into about 8 inch pieces in length.
Slice through the middle, leaving about a ½ inch on each side of loin.
Mix together sausage and salsa.
Stuff loin with mixture.
Marinate in Italian dressing for 1 hour.
Grill on low to medium heat.
The sausage and salsa mixture keeps it from drying out.

ELK SAUSAGE

1 teaspoon onion powder
1 teaspoon garlic powder
1 teaspoon thyme
1 teaspoon red pepper (crushed)
1 teaspoon seasoned salt
1 teaspoon cumin
1 tablespoon sage
1 pound of ground Elk

Mix all of the spices to the one pound of ground Elk and mix well. Make into patties and pan fry.

*Note: When you have your game made into ground meat, you may want to have your local butcher add some pork fat as the Elk is very lean. Another alternative is to just add one tablespoon of oil into the pan before frying.

ANTELOPE JERKY

5 lbs Antelope
1 teaspoon black pepper
1 teaspoon red pepper
1 teaspoon garlic powder
2 tablespoon Blackening spice
4 tablespoon Tomato sauce
2 tablespoon ginger root
¾ cup Worcestershire sauce
¾ cup Soy sauce
Cut meat into ¼ inch thick slices, and then cut into finger size strips.
Combine and mix ingredients and marinate meat strips for 6-8 hours.
Place strips on dehydrator trays and leave for approximately 8-10 hours.
SmokeeJo Tip:
All dehydrators may dry at different times and so it is recommended to check often on the process until you get the time right for your dehydrator.

CHIMICHURRI SAUCE

1 cup fresh Italian parsley
½ cup olive oil
1/3 cup red wine vinegar
¼ cup fresh cilantr –(packed)
2 garlic cloves peeled
¾ teaspoon dried crushed red pepper
½ teaspoon ground cumin
½ teaspoon salt
Puree all ingredients in processor. Transfer to bowl. (This can be made 2 hours ahead. Cover and let stand at room temperature.)
This recipe yields about 1 cup.

GRILLED WILD TURKEY BREAST

1 bone-in wild turkey breast (about 1-1/2 pounds), split
1 bottle (8 oz) Honey Dijon salad dressing
SmokeeJo's Hungarian Game Spice

Place turkey in a large reseal able plastic bag; add salad dressing. Seal bag and turn to coat; refrigerate overnight, turning occasionally.

Drain and discard marinade. Rub the game spice over the turkey breasts evenly and thoroughly. Grill turkey, covered, over indirect medium heat for 45-55 minutes or until juices run clear.

GRILLED BEEF TENDERLOIN

Six 7-ounce beef tenderloin steaks (1 1/2 inches thick)
Coarse sea salt
Chimichurri Sauce

Light a grill; for best flavor, toss a few soaked oak chips onto the fire. Alternatively, preheat a grill pan and oil it lightly. Generously season the steaks with salt and grill over a hot fire for about 8 minutes per side for medium rare. Top each steak with a dollop of Chimichurri sauce.
Recipe to Chimichurri sauce on page 41.

SMOKEEJO'S "SHED SPECIAL" BARBECUE PORK SPARE RIBS

1 Slab of Pork Spare Ribs

Marinade:
12 oz. Bottle of Italian Dressing
¼ cup Worcestershire sauce
¼ cup Dales
1 cup Teriyaki sauce

Mix all of the above ingredients together.
Place ribs in a gallon size Ziploc bag and pour in marinade.
Marinate for 1 hour.

Grill on medium heat for 1 hour.

GRILLED BOSTON BUTT

Medium Boston Butt 4-6 lbs
1 medium onion
4 cloves fresh garlic
Black pepper
Season salt
Worcestershire Sauce
Hungarian Spice –optional
Directions:
With a knife cut small holes in the thick parts of the meat and insert garlic cloves. Sprinkle pepper, seasoned salt, and Hungarian Spice and rub on both sides of the meat.
Sprinkle Worcestershire sauce over meat. Double wrap in foil.
Preheat Grill. Grill on medium to low heat @ 250 to 300 degrees. Turn every 15 to 20 minutes for 1 hour. Remove from foil. Cook on open grill another 30 to 45 turning every 10 minutes until good and brown.

DUCK ON A STICK

4 duck breasts
2 shots of Whiskey
1 lb sliced bacon
Orange Marmalade
Red Wine
SmokeeJo's Hungarian Game Spice (or any seasoning of choice)
Salt
Pepper
Garlic powder
4-6 shish kabob sticks

Blend whiskey with 8 teaspoons of orange marmalade and ½ cup of red wine. Place breasts in dish and cover overnight or at least 6 hours. After marinating, cut duck breasts in bite size pieces and wrap with bacon strips. Put meat on shish kabob sticks and season. Place on grill and baste with left over marinade. Grill about 4 to 6 minutes on each side (depending on thickness of meat). Serve over wild or white rice.

WILD DUCK PERLOW

4 Duck breasts-De-boned and cut into cubes
½ cup salt pork-chopped
1 large onion-chopped
½ Green bell pepper-chopped
4-Cloves garlic-chopped
1 bay leaf
1 tablespoon black pepper
1 tablespoon salt
½ teaspoon thyme
1 cup white (with the white rice I prefer to use jasmine)
1 cup yellow rice
½ cup oil
4 1/2 cups water

In a 6 quart Dutch oven, fry the salt pork in the oil until golden brown.
Remove the salt pork leaving oil.
Add onion, bell pepper, and garlic. Cook about 10 minutes on medium heat, stirring occasionally to keep from sticking. Add the duck and cook for about 4-5 minutes until brown.
Add water and cover with lid and cook on low to med heat until the duck is tender. (About 30 minutes).
Add the rice and bring to a boil stirring once.
Place lid on and cook on low heat for 30 minutes.
Enjoy!

QUAIL AND BROWN RICE

6 quail
Baking bag
1 8oz can of beef consommé
1 small onion diced
2 cloves of garlic (minced)
Salt and pepper
2 cups of long grain brown rice
2 Tablespoon sour cream
2 cups of water

Place quail in baking bag with onion, garlic, and seasonings.
Bake in oven on 350 degrees for 1 hour.
Remove quail from oven and let cool. Save juices from bag and set aside.
Pull meat off of bone.
In stock pot add meat, water, and 1 ½ cups of saved juices from baking bag and brown rice. Bring to a boil. Turn heat down to low, cover and cook for 25 minutes.
Add sour cream and stir well.

STUFFED BARBEQUED QUAIL

4 quail
½ cup gorgonzola cheese
3 tablespoons chopped sun-dried tomatoes previously packed in olive oil
¼ cup fresh basil, minced
Sea salt
Freshly ground black pepper
8 slices of bacon
Extra virgin olive oil for brushing

Preparation:
Prepare the quail stuffing by mixing the cheese, sun-dried tomatoes and basil in a bowl. Season the quail inside and out with salt and pepper before stuffing the quail cavities with the cheese mixture. Close the cavities with toothpicks. Wrap each quail in two pieces of bacon and secure with toothpicks. Brush the quail and the barbeque grill with olive oil before placing the birds on the grill. Cover the grill and cook for approximately ten minutes, during which time you should turn and baste the birds frequently with olive oil. When the quail skin has browned, the meat is cooked but moist inside, and the bacon has turned crisp, the quail should be done.

CAJUN-FRIED QUAIL

2 boneless quail
1 cup buttermilk
2 cups all-purpose flour
1 tablespoon each: garlic powder, chili powder and paprika
1 teaspoon each: cayenne pepper, salt and black pepper
Oil for deep-frying (peanut oil preferred)
Marinate quail in buttermilk 15 minutes in a glass container or plastic bag.
In a small bowl, thoroughly combine flour, garlic powder, chili powder, paprika, cayenne, salt and black pepper; set aside.
Heat oil in a deep-fryer or Dutch oven to 375 degrees. Remove quail from buttermilk and place in flour mixture, turning to coat well. Fry in oil about 8 minutes. Remove and drain on paper towels. Cut in halves.

GRILLED CHUKAR

Six halves of Chukar, skinned
Marinade:
2 cups extra virgin olive oil
1/4 cup red wine vinegar
1/4 cup teriyaki
15 cloves of garlic - coarsely chopped

Soak birds in salt water for 24 hours, changing water every eight hours. Whisk marinade ingredients together well in a glass bowl, add birds. Marinade for 12 to 24 hours, stirring twice. Preheat BBQ grill or prep coals. Drain birds for 15 minutes, reserving marinade for basting. Grill until juices run clear, turning and basting 2 to 3 times. Usually 10-12 minutes. Birds should just start to brown on the breast side. DO NOT OVERCOOK!

HONEY ROASTED PHEASANT

1 pheasant
¾ cup honey
½ cup creamy peanut butter
2 tablespoons cider vinegar
2 tablespoons soy sauce

Combine all ingredients but the pheasant in a medium saucepan. Cook over low heat until peanut butter is melted, stirring frequently.
Place the pheasant in a roasting pan. Pour the sauce over the bird, cover and place into the refrigerator overnight.
Bake at 350 degrees for 1 hour, basting frequently with the drippings.

GRILLED WILD GOOSE

1 Goose
1/2 cup olive oil
1/2 cup soy sauce
1/2 cup brown sugar
1/2 teaspoon Smoked salt
1 teaspoon Garlic powder
1 teaspoon Onion powder
1/2 cup thawed orange juice concentrate
1/2 cup honey Dijon mustard
1/4 cup honey

Mix the oil, soy sauce, brown sugar, seasonings, orange juice and mustard in a bowl. Cut the goose into chunks or slice about 1" thick. Pour the marinade over the goose pieces in a shallow glass pan and marinate for about 4 hours, stirring occasionally. Remove the goose and drain on paper towel. Mix some honey with 1 cup of the reserved marinade. Grill goose pieces over medium heat for approximately 20 minutes. Baste with marinade.

GRILLED JALAPENO DOVE

Ingredients
Fresh Dove Breasts
Bacon
Cheese of your choice (cheddar, Velveeta, or
cream cheese)
Fresh Jalapenos
Lowery's seasoned salt
Tabasco Habanera Sauce

Cooking Instructions:

De-breast the dove so that you have two separate pieces of meat. Marinate meat in Lowery's salt and Tabasco's Habanera Sauce.
Cut the jalapeno peppers in half and de-seed. Fill the pepper with cheese of choice. Place each piece of meat on each side of pepper and wrap with bacon.
Place a toothpick through the bacon & dove and pepper to secure.
You are ready for the grill.

APPETIZERS AND SIDES RECIPES

SMOKEEJO'S FIRECRACKER SKEWERED SHRIMP

2 lbs. raw jumbo shrimp – peeled, de-veined
1 lemon – (juice of)
3 cloves garlic – minced
1 cup olive oil
¼ cup chopped fresh parsley
2 tablespoons Hot sauce
1 tablespoons Tomato paste
2 teaspoon dried oregano
1 teaspoon salt
1 teaspoon black pepper

Combine all ingredients in large plastic zip lock bag.
Marinade at room temperature for 2 hours.
Thread shrimp onto bamboo skewers.
Grill shrimp over medium-low flame for 5 minutes on each side, basting frequently with left over marinade.

STUFFED BACON WRAPPED PRAWNS

1 dozen Prawns (or Large Shrimp)
1 pound of crabmeat
1 pound of bacon
"SmokeeJo's" Blackening Seasoning
Toothpicks (soaked in water for 30 minutes)

Directions:
Prepare your grill to about medium heat.
Split the prawns down the middle being careful not to cut all the way through.
Stuff the middle with just enough crabmeat to fill the cavity.
Take a slice of bacon and wrap completely around the prawn.
Stick a toothpick on each end so that it will stay together securely while grilling.
Sprinkle generously with the blackening seasoning.
Grill over medium coals for 5-10 minutes, turning 2 or 3 times or until the bacon is crispy and browned.
Serve immediately.

WILD RICE & MUSHROOMS

1 cup wild rice
2 tablespoon butter or oil
1 tablespoon grated onion
1 tablespoon each, finely chopped parsley, chives and green pepper
1/2 - lb. fresh mushrooms
Pinch nutmeg
Cook the wild rice as directed. Melt butter, stir in onion, parsley, chives, and green pepper, sauté for three minutes. Add mushrooms, thinly sliced, and cook for 5 minutes over low heat, stirring frequently. Season to taste with salt, pepper and nutmeg. Stir into the cooked, drained wild rice and serve. This can be served as a side dish with any game or meat.

SMOKEEJO'S SPICY CAJUN OYSTERS

2 dozen oysters in the shell, scrubbed
2 cups Spicy Cajun Sauce

Spicy Cajun Sauce:
2 strips of bacon, finely chopped
1 small onion, finely chopped
¾ teaspoon chili powder
¼ teaspoon black pepper
¼ teaspoon ground cumin
1 cup bottled chili sauce (or SmokeeJo's Hot sauce)
2/3 cup orange juice
1/3 cup honey
3 tablespoon cider vinegar
2 large cloves garlic, minced
Cook bacon in saucepan until browned. Drain off and discard fat. Add onion and sauté until tender. Stir in chili powder, pepper and cumin; sauté 1 minute. Add remaining ingredients and cook over low heat, stirring occasionally, for 30 minutes or until sauce is somewhat thickened. This makes 2 cups.

Instructions for Grilling:
Place oysters on non greased grill 4-5 inches over hot coals. Cover with lid or aluminum foil. Cook until oysters begin to open, 5-10 minutes, depending on size. Place on a platter. Open and discard top shells. Spoon a little Spicy Cajun Sauce on to each. Return to the grill and cook, covered, about 2 minutes longer or until sauce bubbles. Serve hot.

GRILLED CRAB BURGERS

6 oz. fresh crabmeat or 1- 6-ounce can; drained
1 1/2 cups fresh white breadcrumbs
1/2 cup chopped green onions
4 1/2 tablespoons mayonnaise
1 teaspoon old bay

1 egg yolk
1 1/2 tablespoon Dijon mustard
1 vegetable oil
 4 large slices French bread

Mix crabmeat, 1 cup breadcrumbs, green onions, 2 tablespoons mayonnaise and Old Bay seasoning in medium bowl. Add the salt and pepper. Mix in egg yolk. Form mixture into four 2 1/2-inch-diameter patties. Place remaining ½ cup breadcrumbs in shallow bowl. Dip patties into crumbs, coating completely. Mix remaining 2 1/2 tablespoons mayonnaise with mustard in small bowl to blend.

Prepare barbecue (medium-high heat) or preheat broiler. Brush barbecue rack with oil. Grill burgers until golden brown, about 4 minutes per side. Grill bread slices until lightly toasted, about 1 minute per side. Spread toasts with mustard dressing. Top each with a burger.

TEMPURA BATTERED SPRING ONIONS

2-3 Bunches of Spring Onions
Tempura Batter
Oil

Cut the green stalks off of the onion leaving about an inch at the end.
Slice the onion down the middle to the stalk being careful not to cut all the way through.
Place the onions in ice water & place in the refrigerator for 30 minutes.
Mix the Tempura batter as directed.
Heat the oil to 350 degrees.
Remove the onion from the ice water and drain well.
Dip onions in Tempura mix.
Drop onion into hot oil and fry until golden brown. Yum, Yum"!!

SMOKEEJO'S TEMPURA BEER BATTER

2 eggs
¾ cup of beer
1 tablespoon Olive oil
1 cup sifted flour
1 tablespoon soy sauce
1 teaspoon mustard
Flour
Separate the eggs, and beat the yolks with the beer, the oil, the flour and the seasonings and blend well. Beat the whites until stiff and fold them in Dip (whatever) in flour and then into the egg batter. Lower then into the frying basket.

VEGGIE'S ON A STICK

1 Green Pepper
1 Red Pepper
8 Medium portabella mushrooms
2 Large sweet onions
3 Yellow squash
3 Zucchini squash
Your favorite Marinade
6-8 shish kabob sticks

Cut all vegetables in bite size pieces.
Slide on sticks. Place on grill and cook
until lightly browned on each side. You
can baste these with your favorite
marinade while grilling.

ST. B'S GREEN BEAN WRAP

Fresh Green Beans
1 lb bacon
Garlic powder
Brown sugar

Directions:
Cut bacon in ½ inch pieces.
Take @ 5-6 green beans and wrap bacon from center.
Place wraps in baking pan.
Coat entire bean wrap with garlic powder.
Sprinkle brown sugar over the top of wraps.
Cover *TIGHTLY with aluminum foil.
*Bake @ 350 degrees for 1 hour.

GRILLED ASPARAGUS

Ingredients:
2 pounds asparagus, cleaned, tough ends removed
Salt and pepper to taste
Flavored olive oil

Heat grill to medium-high heat. Add the asparagus, in batches, and grill until just tender, turning occasionally to get all sides, about 10 minutes. Sprinkle with garlic-flavored olive oil and salt and pepper.

GRILLED SUMMER SQUASH

6 yellow squash cut into 2 x ¼ inch strips
6 zucchini cut into 2 x ¼ inch strips
Minced garlic
Olive Oil
Heavy duty aluminum foil

Arrange squash on aluminum foil and sprinkle over the tops with olive oil and minced garlic.
Wrap in aluminum foil.
Grill for 15-20 minutes.

GRILLED TOMATOES

Ingredients:
Tomatoes
Grated Parmesan cheese
Margarine or butter

To Prepare:
Cut a thin slice from stem ends of tomatoes. Sprinkle tomatoes with cheese; dot with margarine. Place tomatoes on cooking grill. Cover and grill until heated through, 10-15 minutes.

BOURBON BAKED BEANS

Four 16-oz. jars or cans of baked beans
One 15-oz. can crushed pineapple, drained
One 12-oz jar chili sauce
½ cup strong brewed coffee
½ cup bourbon
¼ cup firmly packed brown sugar
1 tablespoon molasses
¾ teaspoon dry mustard

Slow cooker:2-3 hours

Combine canned baked beans in a large slow cooker with drained pineapple, chili sauce, coffee, bourbon, brown sugar, molasses and dry mustard. Stir well, cover and cook on high for 2 hours. Uncover, stir and cook to desired consistency. This takes another hour or so and beans may still be runnier than you like. If so, transfer beans to a large skillet or Dutch oven and simmer, uncovered, to proper consistency, or serve with a slotted spoon.

CAJUN GRILLED CORN ON THE COB

Ingredients:
6 ears corn, husked and cleaned
½ cup butter, softened
6 tablespoons SmokeeJo's Blackening Seasoning

Directions:

Peel back husks from the corn, remove strings and leave just a few layers of husk on the corn.

Spread butter or margarine over each ear of corn. Sprinkle seasoning lightly over each ear, or to taste. Fold corn husks back over the corn. Wrap in foil.

Place on grill for 25 minutes, turning occasionally. Unwrap foil, peel back husks and enjoy.

Makes 6 servings

GRILLED CARROTS & ONIONS

1 lb. small carrots, peeled
½ cup red onion, chopped
4 teaspoons butter
2 teaspoons fresh thyme, chopped or ½ dried thyme
Salt & pepper to taste

Divide carrots between two pieces of foil large enough to fold into packets. Sprinkle evenly with onion, butter and thyme: season with salt and pepper to taste. Loosely wrap foil over vegetables, sealing tightly. Place on grill over medium-high heat: cook, turning once, for 20 to 25 minutes or until tender-crisp.

GRILLED POTATOES

8 potatoes, pared
2 onions, thinly sliced 1/4' thick
1 tablespoon fresh parsley, chopped
1 1/2 teaspoons salt
fresh ground black pepper
1/4 cup margarine
1 cup beef stock, hot

Mix potatoes and onions. Sprinkle evenly with parsley, salt & pepper. Spread 1/2 deep in buttered aluminum foil pan. Dot with margarine or butter. Add hot stock. Place on grill on indirect heat, cover and bake 30 to 40 minutes until potatoes are tender, brown and crusty and the liquid has disappeared.

DEEP FRIED SWEET POTATOES

3 large sweet potatoes
Canola, peanut or vegetable oil
Deep fryer or pan
Salt to taste

Peel potatoes. Cut each in 1/2-inch slices. Then cut slices into 1/4-inch sticks. Place in a bowl of ice water to soak for 30 minutes. Heat the oil to 360* in deep fryer. Drain potatoes and pat dry thoroughly using paper towels to avoid the oil from splattering with any excess water.
Dip frying basket in oil (this prevents the potatoes from sticking to it), then add a handful of potatoes into basket. Lower into oil and-fry for 3 minutes or until potatoes are tender, but not browned. Lift basket and allow potatoes to drain. Pour onto double paper towels. Repeat procedure with remaining potatoes.
Increase the temperature of the heated oil to 390 degrees
Return the fried potatoes to the oil in batches and cook a second time until golden and crispy.

GRILLED COLE SLAW

1 Head Green Cabbage, Cored
½ cup White Vinegar
½ cup brown sugar
2 tablespoons olive oil
1 tablespoon cracked black pepper
Salt to taste

Cut the head of cabbage into 6 wedges and place on the grill. Cook the cabbage wedges on each of the 3 sides for 3 minutes per side. Remove from grill and shred.

Mix the remaining ingredients together and toss with the shredded cabbage.

GRILLED POTATO SKINS

6 Baking potatoes
2 tablespoons margarine or butter, melted
½ cup picante sauce
1 cup shredded cheddar cheese
3 slices bacon, crisp and crumbled
Chopped tomato
Sliced green onion
½ cup sour cream

Scrub potatoes. Wrap each potato in heavy foil. Prick with a fork. Grill over medium coals for 1-2 hours until tender. Unwrap potatoes and cool.
Cut potatoes in half lengthwise. Scoop out potato pulp, leaving ¼ inch thick shell. Brush the inside of each potato shell with melted butter. Spoon 2 teaspoons picante sauce into each potato shell. Sprinkle

each with cheese. Add bacon. Grill potato skins on an uncovered grill directly over medium coals for 10-15 minutes or until skins are crisp. Sprinkle with tomato and green onion. Top with sour cream. Makes 12 potato skins.

*Note: To prepare ahead of time you can bake the potatoes in the oven at 400 degrees for 1 hour or until tender. Scoop out potato pulp as above and place the skins in the refrigerator covered until ready to take to the grill. Grill as above directions (10-15 minutes). They will still have that grilled flavor and can be cooked along with steaks or chops.

"SPICED UP" GRILLED PINEAPPLE

1 large pineapple peeled, cored, cut into 2x1 inch pieces
¾ cup Tequila
¾ cup (packed) golden brown sugar
1and 1/2 teaspoons vanilla extract
¼ teaspoon ground cinnamon
6 bamboo skewers, soaked in water 30 minutes drained
Stir first 4 ingredients in small bowl until sugar dissolves.
Thread pineapple pieces onto 6 skewers, dividing equally.

Prepare barbecue (medium heat). Grill pineapple until brown, basting with tequila mixture and turning occasionally, about 10 minutes total.
Remove pineapple from skewer; serve hot or warm.

CAMP FIRE COBBLER

1 package yellow or white cake mix (as directed on package)
1 can crushed pineapple
1 can raspberry pie filling
Fresh blueberries (or your preference)
1 stick of butter
Charcoal

Have your coals good and hot, they should be white. You will need 8 coals on the bottom & 17 on the top, distributed evenly. *You will want to have some extra coals to replace the ones that go out faster than others.*
Pour cans of filling and pineapple in bottom of Dutch oven.Pour cake mix over the top of fruit.
DO NOT STIR!
Cut up your butter into squares and evenly place on top of cake mixture.
Sprinkle fresh blueberries all over the top.
After 10 minutes of cooking without lifting the lid, you will need to spin the lid ¼ of a turn, and then the whole oven ¼ of a turn. You will repeat this again after another 10 minutes.
You will do this again twice more.
Total cooking time is 45 minutes.

Enjoy!

Some of my favorite spices

ALLSPICE
Uses: <u>WHOLE-</u> Pickles, meats, boiled fish, gravies. <u>GROUND-</u>Puddings, relishes, fruit preserves, baking. Good on just about everything!

BASIL
Uses: For flavoring tomato dishes and tomato paste, also use in cooked peas, squash, snap beans; sprinkle on poultry and game.

BAY LEAVES
Uses: For pickling, stews, for spicing sauces and soup. Also use with a variety of meats and fish.

DILL
Uses: Dill is a predominant seasoning in pickling recipes; also adds pleasing flavor to grilled fish recipes, and I particularly like to use it in my fish batters.

OREGANO
Uses: An excellent flavoring for any tomato dish, and Italian specialties, such as Lasagna & Spaghetti. Blended with other Italian seasonings makes a great rub for grilled fish!

PAPRIKA
Uses: A colorful garnish for pale foods, and for seasoning goulash, and salads. It adds great flavoring to potato salad!

ROSEMARY
Uses: In soups, stews and to sprinkle on beef. When fresh, adds a wonderful flavor topped on grilled fish.

SAGE
Uses: For meat and poultry stuffing, <u>sausages,</u> and salads. It will add a flavorful taste in your beef stews.

THYME
Uses: For poultry seasoning, in croquettes and fish dishes. It adds an excellent flavor to beef and game. I particularly like to use it in my venison stews.

Emergency Substitutions

1/4 Dry Bread Crumbs = ¼ cup cracker crumbs, 1 slice of bread cubed, 2/3 cup rolled oats

1 cup Buttermilk = 1 tablespoon vinegar plus milk to make 1 cup

½ Cup Corn Syrup = ½ cup sugar plus 2 tablespoons liquid

1 egg = 2 egg yolks, When baking, add 1 tablespoon of water

1 Clove Garlic = 1/8 teaspoon instant minced garlic or garlic powder, or ½ teaspoon of garlic salt

2 tablespoons Green or Red Pepper = 1 tablespoon sweet pepper flakes

1 tablespoon Herbs, Fresh = 1 teaspoon dried herbs

1 cup Honey = 1 1/4 cups sugar plus ¼ cup liquid

1 teaspoon Lemon or Orange Peel = ½ teaspoon dried peel

1 small (1/4 cup) Onion = 1 tablespoon instant minced onion or onion Flakes, ¼ cup frozen chopped onion, or 1 Teaspoon onion powder